Stage 4
More Stories C
Pam Mayo

Group/Guided Reading Notes

Contents

Introduction	2
Comprehension strategies	3
Vocabulary and phonic opportunities	4
Curriculum coverage chart	5

Dad's Jacket
Group or guided reading	8
Group and independent reading activities	9
Speaking, listening and drama activities	10
Writing activities	11

Stuck in the Mud
Group or guided reading	12
Group and independent reading activities	13
Speaking, listening and drama activities	15
Writing activities	15

The Den
Group or guided reading	16
Group and independent reading activities	17
Speaking, listening and drama activities	19
Writing activities	19

Look Smart
Group or guided reading	20
Group and independent reading activities	21
Speaking, listening and drama activities	22
Writing activities	23

Tug of War
Group or guided reading	24
Group and independent reading activities	25
Speaking, listening and drama activities	26
Writing activities	27

An Important Case
Group or guided reading	28
Group and independent reading activities	29
Speaking, listening and drama activities	31
Writing activities	31

Introduction

Oxford Reading Tree stories at Stages 1–4 feature settings and situations most children will find familiar. The stories reflect the experiences of most 4–6-year-olds: having a bath, going to a party, having new shoes, getting into trouble. Children of this age will readily identify with the characters and situations. This also helps build comprehension.

Each book tells a complete story, using natural language, phonically decodable words and high frequency words, all supported by funny and engaging pictures. The books offer plenty of scope for developing children's word recognition and language comprehension skills. When used alongside your systematic phonic teaching they will help children put all their reading skills into practice in a highly motivating way.

Using the books

This booklet provides suggestions for using the books for guided, group and independent activities. The reading activities include ideas for developing children's *word recognition* **W** and *language comprehension* **C** skills. Within word recognition, there are ideas for helping children practise their phonic skills and knowledge, as well as helping them to tackle words that are not easy to decode phonically. The language comprehension ideas include suggestions for teaching the skills of prediction, questioning, clarifying, summarising and imagining in order to help children understand the text and the whole stories. Suggestions are also provided for speaking, listening, drama and writing activities.

Reading fluency

To support children in developing fluency in their reading, and give them plenty of opportunities to revisit the stories. This includes:
- rereading independently
- rereading with a partner
- rereading at home
- listening to audio versions of the story (e.g. Talking Stories)
- hearing the story read to them by others as they follow the printed text.

Rereading and rehearing helps children develop automatic word recognition and gives them models of fluent, expressive reading.

Comprehension strategies

Story	Comprehension strategies taught through these Group/Guided Reading Notes				
	Prediction	Questioning	Clarifying	Summarising	Imagining
Dad's Jacket	✓	✓	✓	✓	✓
Stuck in the Mud	✓	✓	✓	✓	
The Den		✓	✓	✓	✓
Look Smart		✓	✓	✓	✓
Tug of War	✓	✓	✓		✓
An Important Case	✓	✓	✓	✓	✓

Vocabulary and phonic opportunities

The chart shows the main words used in each book. The decodable words listed should be decodable for most children at this Stage. The tricky words are common but do not conform to the phonic rules taught up to this point – children will need support to learn and recognise them. If children struggle with one of these words you can model how to read it.

Dad's Jacket	Decodable words	after, books, children, five, game, good, help, invented, jacket, made, man, need, plants, put (north), sorry, stop, ten, that
	Tricky words	bought, clothes, have, idea, outside, poster, pounds, some, tables, wanted
Stuck in the Mud	Decodable words	boot, children, deep, got, help, inside, lead, lost, muddy, path, sank, sheep, stuck, that, too
	Tricky words	couldn't, do, hair, knees, out, pulled, pushed, their, walk, were, what, where
The Den	Decodable words	back, began, but, by, children, logs, made, make, nest, next, put (north), rain, sticks, stop, stream, them, time, week
	Tricky words	asked, branches, couldn't, everyone, found, idea, some, splashed, stopped, straw, swan, wanted
Look Smart	Decodable words	been, dress, good, job, lipstick, lorry, muddy, nobody, off, put (north), shopping, splash, this, tray
	Tricky words	chocolate, new, over, party, paws, shirt, smart, some, want, what
Tug of War	Decodable words	began, by, children, fell, jump, rope, skip, stream, tied, too, tree, whoops
	Tricky words	bridge, easy, found, idea, over, park, pull, threw
An Important Case	Decodable words	but, case, children, important, landed, sandwiches, sorry, thank, that, took, very
	Tricky words	asked, ball, bush, couldn't, don't, football, found, kicked, know, open, outside, police officer, small, were, what

Curriculum coverage chart

	Speaking, listening, drama	Reading	Writing
Dad's Jacket			
PNS Literacy Framework (Y1)	1.3, 4.1, 4.2	**W** 6.2, 6.3 **C** 7.1, 7.4	9.1, 9.2
National Curriculum	Working within Level 1		
Scotland (5–14) (P2)	Level A	Level A	Level A
N. Ireland (P2/Y2)	Social Use of Language: 6 Language and Thinking: 4, 5, 11	1, 2, 3, 4, 5, 6	2, 3, 4
Wales (Key Stage 1)	Range: 5 Skills: 1, 2,	Range: 1, 2, 4, 5, 6 Skills: 1, 2	Range: 1, 3, 4 Skills: 1, 2, 6
Stuck in the Mud			
PNS Literacy Framework (Y1)	1.2	**W** 5.1, 5.4, 5.5, 5.6 **C** 7.1, 7.2,	10.2
National Curriculum	Working within Level 1		
Scotland (5–14) (P2)	Level A	Level A	Level A
N. Ireland (P2/Y2)	Language and Thinking: 1, 4, 11	1, 2, 3, 4, 5, 6, 7	3
Wales (Key Stage 1)	Range: 1, 2 Skills: 1, 2, 3	Range: 1, 2, 4, 5, 6 Skills: 1, 2	Range: 1, 2, 3, 4, 6 Skills: 1, 2, 6, 8

Key

C = Language comprehension   Y = Year
W = Word recognition   P = Primary

In the designations such as 5.2, the first number represents the strand and the second number the bullet point

Curriculum coverage chart

	Speaking, listening, drama	Reading	Writing
The Den			
PNS Literacy Framework (Y1)	2.2	**W** 5.5, 6.2, 6.3 **C** 7.2, 7.3	9.2, 11.1
National Curriculum	Working within Level 1		
Scotland (5–14) (P2)	Level A	Level A	Level A
N. Ireland (P2/Y2)	Language and Thinking: 5, 8, 11	1, 2, 3, 4, 5, 6	3
Wales (Key Stage 1)	Range: 2, 3 Skills: 1, 3, 5	Range: 1, 2, 4, 5, 6 Skills: 1, 2	Range: 1, 3, 4, 6 Skills: 1, 5, 8
Look Smart			
PNS Literacy Framework (Y1)	1.2, 2.1, 3.2	**W** 5.2, 5.5, 6.2, 6.3 **C** 7.2	10.1, 11.1, 12.2
National Curriculum	Working within Level 1		
Scotland (5–14) (P2)	Level A	Level A	Level A
N. Ireland (P2/Y2)	Language and Thinking: 4, 5, 11	1, 2, 3, 4, 5, 6	3, 6
Wales (Key Stage 1)	Range: 1, 2, 3 Skills: 1, 2, 5, 6	Range: 1, 2, 4, 5, 6 Skills: 1, 2	Range: 1, 3, 4 Skills: 1, 2, 6

Curriculum coverage chart

	Speaking, listening, drama	Reading	Writing
Tug of War			
PNS Literacy Framework (Y1)	4.1, 4.2	W 5.5, 6.2, 6.3 C 7.3	11.1, 11.2, 12.1
National Curriculum	Working within Level 1		
Scotland (5–14) (P2)	Level A	Level A	Level A
N. Ireland (P2/Y2)	Social Use of Language: 6 Language and Thinking: 4, 5	1, 2, 3, 4, 5, 6	3
Wales (Key Stage 1)	Range: 1, 2, 3, 5 Skills: 1, 2, 5	Range: 1, 2, 4, 5, 6 Skills: 1, 2	Range: 1, 3, 4 Skills: 1, 2, 6, 8
An Important Case			
PNS Literacy Framework (Y1)	1.1, 1.3, 3.1	W 5.3, 5.5, 6.1 C 7.2, 8.2	11.1, 11.2, 12.1
National Curriculum	Working within Level 1		
Scotland (5–14) (P2)	Level A	Level A	Level A
N. Ireland (P2/Y2)	Language and Thinking: 10, 11	1, 2, 3, 4, 5, 6, 7	3, 4
Wales (Key Stage 1)	Range: 1, 3 Skills: 1, 2, 3, 4, 5, 6	Range: 1, 2, 4, 5, 6 Skills: 1, 2	Range: 1, 3, 4 Skills: 1, 2, 3, 7

Dad's Jacket

> **C** = Language comprehension   **R, AF** = QCA reading assessment focus
> **W** = Word recognition   **W, AF** = QCA writing assessment focus

Group or guided reading

Introducing the book

C *(Clarifying)* Ask the children if they have heard of the Children in Need appeal. Find out whether they have seen any television programmes. If necessary, explain that Children in Need raises money to help children all over the world.

C *(Questioning, Prediction)* Read the title, pointing to the words, and look at the picture. Ask: *Who is in the picture? What do you think is going to happen in this story?*

W Look at pages 4 and 5 and name the things that the children are hoping to sell. Find the words 'books', 'clothes' and 'plants' in the text.

Strategy check

Remind the children to use their knowledge of fund-raising to help them understand what is happening in the story.

Independent reading

- Ask the children to read the book on their own from the beginning. Listen to each child in turn. Remind them to use a bookmark or card under the line of text to help them keep their place.

W Encourage the children to sound out new CVC words. Prompt if you need to but give praise for reading fluently and with expression.

C *(Clarifying)* Talk about the events on each page as the child reads. Encourage them to take time to explore and talk about the pictures.

(W) Tell them: *When you meet new words, look for familiar phonemes and vowel sounds,* e.g. 'ck' in 'jacket', and 'ou' in 'outside' and 'pounds'.

Assessment Check that the children:
- *(R, AF1)* use a variety of strategies when they meet new vocabulary
- *(R, AF1)* can identify separate phonemes within words.

Returning to the text

(C) *(Questioning, Clarifying)* Ask: *How did the story begin?* Ask the children to explain why the children in the story were having a sale. Ask: *What were they selling?*

(C) *(Questioning, Clarifying)* Read the story up to page 5. Compare the story with the children's version. Ask: *Are they the same? In what way are they different?*

(C) *(Questioning)* Look at pages 6–7 and ask: *What is happening in the picture but is not in the written story?*

(C) *(Imagining)* Return to pages 10–11. Ask: *How do you think Dad felt when he couldn't find his jacket? How would you feel if you lost something? How do you think Wilma felt?*

Group and independent reading activities

Objective Identify the main events and characters in stories, and find specific information in simple texts (7.1). Interpret a text by reading aloud with some variety in pace and emphasis (1.3).

(C) *(Summarising, Clarifying)* Ask: *How did Dad lose his jacket?* Ask the children to retell the story.

- Ask children to take turns to read parts of the story to check whether the retelling was accurate. Do they notice that the told version was different from the book?

Assessment *(R, AF2)* Do the children retell the story in the correct sequence?

Dad's Jacket

Objective Recognise the main elements that shape different texts (7.4).

- **(W)** Ask the children to look at pages 2–3. Ask: *How many sentences are there on these pages?*
- Ask one child to tell you the first word in the sentence on page 2. Then ask the children: *What is the last word in this sentence?*
- Play a game in which children choose a page and then ask another child to find a sentence that begins or ends with a certain word, e.g. *On page 5, can you find a sentence that ends with 'plants'?*

Assessment *(R, AF2)* Do the children know where a sentence begins and ends?

Objective Segment sounds into their constituent phonemes in order to spell them correctly (6.2). Children move from spelling simple CVC words to longer words that include common diagraphs and adjacent consonants (6.3).

- **(W)** Ask the children to look through the story and find the longest words. Count the letters and agree which are the longest ('children', 'invented', 'outside', 'clothes', 'Anneena'). Write these words on the board.
- Ask a child to choose one of the words and tell you all the phonemes. Write the word again, showing the phonemes, e.g. 'ch-i-l-d-r-e-n'.
- **(G)** Repeat with all the words in the list, asking a different child to say the phonemes each time. Ask the group to write 'children' and 'invented' on their whiteboards.

Assessment *(R, AF1)* Were the children able to recognise all the phonemes in each word?

Speaking, listening and drama activities

Objective Explore familiar themes and characters through improvisation and role-play (4.1). Act out stories, using voices for characters (4.2).

- Reread pages 8–16. Ask: *Who sold dad's jacket?*

Dad's Jacket

- Ask volunteers to be Wilma, Dad and the man. Ask them to mime this part of the story: Wilma helps the man try on the jacket; he pays for it; Dad chases the man and gets the jacket; Dad gives money to the man; the man gives the money to Wilma.
- Look back at the book to find out what the characters say. Ask the children to suggest voices for Dad and the man.
- Ask volunteers to think about their characters and then to act out the story with dialogue this time.

Writing activities

Objective Identify the main events and characters in stories, and find specific information in simple texts (7.1). Independently choose what to write about, plan and follow it through (9.1). Use key features of narrative in their own writing (9.2).

- Explain that you would like the children to retell the main parts of this story in a sequence of four pictures.
- Ask the children to tell you the main events of the story. Make a list on the board for the children to refer to later.
- Ask them to choose four main events from the list to retell the story. Ask the children to write speech bubbles or captions to portray what happened in each event.
- Ask the children to use their pictures to retell the story orally to the class.

Assessment *(W, AF2)* Could the children use their speech bubbles effectively to retell their stories?

Stuck in the Mud

C = Language comprehension   **R, AF** = QCA reading assessment focus
W = Word recognition   **W, AF** = QCA writing assessment focus

Group or guided reading

Introducing the book

- **(C)** *(Questioning)* Talk about the picture on the cover. Notice the jackets the children are wearing. Ask: *Can you guess what the weather is like? What time of the year might it be?*

- **(C)** *(Questioning, Prediction)* Read the title and what it says about the story on the back cover. Ask: *What do you think will happen in this story?*

- Read the word list on the back cover together. Check that the children recognise all the words.

Strategy check
Remind the children about question marks when they appear.

Independent reading

- Ask the children to read the book on their own from the beginning. Listen to each child in turn.

- **(W)** Encourage the children to sound out new CVC words. Praise them for reading with appropriate expression but prompt if necessary.

- **(C)** *(Clarifying)* Encourage the children to use the pictures to help them understand the story.

- **(C)** *(Questioning)* On pages 3 and 4, ask the children to point to the question marks. Ask: *How would you read this sentence?* Praise them for reading questions with appropriate expression.

- **(C)** *(Summarising)* Ask children to retell the story in just two or three sentences.

Assessment Check that children:

- *(R, AF1)* use a range of strategies, including the pictures, to work out new words
- *(R, AF3)* read aloud using expression appropriate to the grammar of the text.

Returning to the text

- 🅒 *(Questioning, Clarifying)* On page 5, ask: *Why did Dad say, "Put Floppy on a lead"?*
- 🅒 *(Questioning)* Ask: *Who pushed and pulled to get the sheep out of the mud?*
- 🅒 *(Summarising)* Ask the children to describe the events that led to Dad getting stuck in the mud.

Group and independent reading activities

Objective Retell stories, ordering events using story language (1.2). Read more challenging texts which can be decoded using phonic knowledge and skills, along with automatic recognition of high frequency words (5.6). Identify the main events and characters in stories (7.1).

- 🅒 *(Questioning, Summarising)* **You will need** copies of other stories that the children have read recently.
- Talk about this story and ask the children to tell you how it ends.
- Read pages 14–16 again. Ask: *Does this tell us what happened, or is it a joke? Do you think this is a good way to end a story?*
- Choose another Oxford Reading Tree book and ask: *Do you remember how this story ends?* Read the last two pages of the book to find out.
- Ask the children to tell you about stories they know that ended with an 'Oh no!' joke, e.g. 'Nobody Got Wet' (Stage 4 More Stories A) or 'Everyone Got Wet' (Stage 4 More Stories B).
- Find some stories with happy endings, e.g. 'Poor Old Mum' (Stage 4 More Stories A), 'Swap' (Stage 4 More Stories B).

Assessment *(R, AF3)* Are the children able to see similarities and differences in the story endings?

Objective Recognise and use alternative ways of pronouncing the graphemes already taught (5.1). Use syntax and context when reading for meaning (7.2).

- Ⓦ Use reusable stickers to cover some words, e.g. 'muddy' (page 2), 'asked' (page 3), 'lead' (page 5), 'deep' (page 7).
- Read the book together. When you get to a covered word ask the children to guess what the word might be. Say the whole sentence, putting in one of their suggested words. Praise the children for suggesting words that make sense.
- Partly peel back the sticker to reveal the initial letter of the missing word. Ask the children: *Does the letter match any of the words we thought it might be?*
- Reveal the whole word and read the whole sentence.
- Repeat with other words in the story.

Assessment *(R, AF1)* Did the children suggest words that made sense?

Objective Recognise automatically an increasing number of familiar high frequency words (5.4).

- Ⓦ Play a game using the list of high frequency words on the back cover of the book.
- Choose one of the words, e.g. 'what', and a child to look through the book to find the word. The child tells everyone which page to look at. Ask all the children to point to the word.
- Ask the child who found the page to choose the next person. The adult tells the child which word to search for. Repeat until you have found all the words listed.

Assessment Do the children find the high frequency words quickly?

Speaking, listening and drama activities

Objective Retell stories, ordering events using story language (1.2).

- **You will need** one copy of the book with the text covered.
- Ask the children if they have ever been on a muddy walk. Can they remember how it felt? Ask them to imagine the mud as they do this activity.
- Ask a child to tell you how the story begins. Reword what the child says, if necessary, to use the past tense.
- Continue through the book, with a different child telling what happened on each double-page spread.
- Praise the children for using story language and using the past tense to retell the story.

Writing activities

Objective Apply phonic knowledge and skills as the prime approach to reading and spelling unfamiliar words that are not completely decodable (5.5). Group written sentences together in chunks of meaning or subject (10.2).

- Explain to the children that they are going to write their own version of this story. Retell the story together before the children begin to write.
- Then ask them to write without referring to the book. Remind them to use their knowledge of letter sounds to spell new words.
- Select some words that several children have misspelled. Talk about the right way to spell these words, drawing attention to phonemes and letter strings.

Assessment *(W, AF8)* Check that the children are using phonic strategies to work out how to write unfamiliar words.

The Den

- **C** = Language comprehension
- **W** = Word recognition
- **R, AF** = QCA reading assessment focus
- **W, AF** = QCA writing assessment focus

Group or guided reading

Introducing the book

- **C** *(Clarifying)* Ask the children to tell you what a den is. Talk about dens they might have made – under tables or in their gardens.
- **C** *(Clarifying)* Look through the pictures to find out where the children make a den in this story.
- Read the sentence about the story on the back cover.

Strategy check

Remind the children to use the pictures to help them read unfamiliar words.

Independent reading

- Ask the children to read the book on their own from the beginning. Listen to each child in turn.
- **W** Encourage the children to sound out new CVC words. Praise them for reading with expression.
- **C** *(Summarising)* Ask children to retell the story in a few sentences.

Assessment (R, AF1) Do the children remember the key points of the story (building a den, the rain, the surprise when they went back)?

Returning to the text

- **C** *(Clarifying)* Encourage the children to reread a sentence if they miss a word or if it does not seem to make sense.

- **(W)** Praise them for using phonemes and the sense of the sentence to work out new words.
- **(C)** *(Questioning)* Ask the children what is happening in some of the pictures to check their understanding.
- **(C)** *(Imagining)* Discuss how Wilma might have felt when she looked into the den on page 15.

Assessment Check that the children:

- *(R, AF1)* automatically blend consonants such as 'st', 'tw' and 'str' when reading
- *(R, AF1)* check for sense by rereading sentences.

Group and independent reading activities

Objective Apply phonic knowledge and skills as the prime approach to reading words (5.5). Segment sounds into their constituent phonemes (6.2). Children move from spelling simple CVC words to longer words (6.3).

- **(W)** Demonstrate how you would work out a word such as 'straw', using phonemes, the picture and the sense of the story.
- Ask the children to choose a word that they think other children might find hard to read, e.g. 'stream', 'idea', 'found'.
- Ask each child to explain how to read the word they chose from the book. Praise them for using as many clues as possible.

Assessment *(R, AF1)* Check that the children are aware that they can use a variety of approaches including decoding to read new words.

Objective Use syntax and context when reading for meaning (7.2).

- **(W) You will need** a copy of the book with some words covered with reusable stickers. Write substitute words (that look similar but do not make sense) on the stickers, e.g. page 1: change 'by' to 'be'.

- Ask a different child to read each page. Ask them to say what is wrong with the sentence. Ask them to suggest what the real word should be. Peel away the sticker to check.

Assessment *(R, AF1)* Check that the children are aware that the sentence does not make sense. Do they suggest a word that would put it right?

Objective Recognise automatically an increasing number of familiar high frequency words (5.4).

(W) Look at the title on the cover of the book. Ask the children: *Can you find a word inside the word 'the'?* Praise them for finding 'he'.

Go through the book and on each page ask the children to put their hands up when they see a small word inside a longer one, e.g. page 1: 'child' in 'children', 'we' in 'were', 'am' in 'stream'.

Assessment *(R, AF1)* Do the children find the shorter words quickly?

Objective Segment sounds into their constituent phonemes in order to spell them correctly (6.2). Children move from spelling simple CVC words to longer words (6.3).

(W) Write the following words on the board: 'sticks', 'branches', 'children', 'splashed'.

- Together, let the children read them by sounding out the phonemes.
- Clean the board and ask them to write the words on their whiteboards as you call them out. Say each word twice, very clearly, sounding out the phonemes carefully, but not unnaturally.

Assessment *(W, AF8)* Check that the children include all the adjacent consonants, e.g. 'cks' in 'sticks' and 'ldr' in 'children'.

Objective Make predictions showing an understanding of ideas, events and characters (7.3).

(C) *(Questioning)* Ask the children to look at the cover of the book. Now that they know the story, can they suggest why the illustrator has put a swan in the picture?

Assessment *(R, AF3)* Check that the children realise that the swan on the cover is a clue to the end of the story. This will help them in their own writing.

Speaking, listening and drama activities

Objective Listen to and follow instructions accurately (2.2).

- Give each child a pencil and paper and tell them that you are going to give them instructions for drawing the den in the story.
- Tell them what to do step by step: *Draw a long stick with a fork at the top. Draw two more long sticks leaning against this stick.*
- Continue with the instructions, following the sequence of building the den in the story, finishing with: *Draw a swan on a nest in the den.*
- Let the children take turns, one child giving the others instructions on, e.g., 'How to draw a house', 'How to draw a man', 'How to draw a face'.

Writing activities

Objective Use key features of narrative in their own writing (9.2). Compose and write simple sentences independently to communicate meaning (11.1).

- Talk about the story with the children. Make a list of the main points: Wilf's idea, making the den, the rain, the swan.
- Ask the children to think of something they might make with their friends, e.g. a camp, a circuit for their bikes.
- Ask them to imagine that there is a reason why they do not go back to it for some time, e.g. they go on holiday, it rains, or they are unwell.
- Ask them to think of something that might have happened in the meantime, e.g. other children have used it for something else; builders have moved in. Ask the children: *How do you think this story will end?*
- Ask each child to write their own story using their suggestions.

Assessment *(W, AF3)* Do the children use the story structure (beginning, middle, end) to write their story? Do they ask for help when they get stuck?

Look Smart

C = Language comprehension   **R, AF** = QCA reading assessment focus
W = Word recognition   **W, AF** = QCA writing assessment focus

Group or guided reading

Introducing the book

C *(Questioning, Prediction)* Look at the picture on the cover and read the title. Ask: *Who do you think looks smart? Can anyone suggest where the family might be going?*

- Read the sentence about the story on the back cover.
- **W** Check that everyone can read the high frequency words listed on the back cover.

Strategy check

Remind the children that some words on the back cover need to be learned as they cannot all be decoded: 'some', 'want', 'what'.

Independent reading

- Ask the children to read the book on their own from the beginning. Listen to each child in turn. Remind them to use a card under the line of text to help them keep their place.
- **W** Encourage the children to sound out new CVC words. Praise them for reading fluently with expression.
- **C** *(Summarising)* Ask children to retell the story in just two or three sentences.

Assessment Check that the children:
- *(R, AF1)* read the high frequency words without difficulty
- *(R, AF3)* notice where sentences begin and end, and use appropriate expression.

Returning to the text

C *(Questioning, Clarifying)* Talk about the story and the new clothes.

W Ask the children to find the word 'been' on page 1. Can they find other words with the same 'ee' sound but with a different spelling? (m<u>e</u>, Flopp<u>y</u>, mudd<u>y</u>, h<u>e</u>, part<u>y</u>, lorr<u>y</u>) Point out that not all words ending in 'y' have an 'ee' sound (e.g. my, by).

C *(Clarifying)* Ask: *Do you like having new clothes? Do you like looking smart?*

C *(Questioning)* Look at pages 2 and 4, and then look at page 24. Ask: *Do you think Biff likes wearing a dress?* (She looks much happier on page 24.)

C *(Imagining)* Ask the children to think about how they would feel if they were given some new clothes to wear. Would they be pleased with the gift, or would they be cross that they didn't choose the clothes for themselves?

C *(Clarifying)* Look at the pictures on pages 10, 12, 14, 16, and 22. Ask: *How do you think Mum felt? Do you sometimes feel like this?*

Group and independent reading activities

Objective Recognise and use alternative ways of spelling the phonemes already taught (5.2). Segment sounds into their constituent phonemes in order to spell them correctly (6.2). Children move from simple CVC words to longer words (6.3).

- Ask the children to find 'shirt' on page 3. Ask a child to tell the group all the phonemes in the word. Write the word on a board showing the phonemes: 'sh–ir–t'. Ask: *What would the word be if we took away 'sh' and used 'd' instead? Who had a dirty shirt in the story?*

- Ask the children to find 'smart' on page 5. Ask a child to say all the phonemes. Write the word on the board: 's–m–ar–t'. Ask: *What would the word be if it began with 'st' instead of 'sm'? Did the children look smart at the start of the story?*

Look Smart

- Find the phonemes in 'paws' on page 16. Ask the children to say the word that we get if we change 'p' to 'j'. Ask: *Was it Floppy's paws or his jaws that spoilt Chip's shirt?*

Assessment (R, AF1) Could the children identify the phonemes and use the spelling patterns to make new words?

Objective Use syntax when reading for meaning (7.2).

C *(Questioning)* Ask the children to look through the story and find the longest sentence in the book (page 3). Ask: *How do we know where a sentence begins and ends?*

Ask the children to find any page that has speech marks. Ask: *How many sentences are there?* Ask a volunteer to read the sentences.

Assessment (R, AF1) When the children read, do they show by their expression that they know where the sentence ends?

Objective Apply phonic knowledge and skills as the prime approach to reading and spelling unfamiliar words (5.5).

W List the following words from the story on the board: 'had', 'top', 'bag', 'mud', 'job'.

Tell the children you are going to play a guessing game. You will give them clues about a word. When they have three clues, they may guess the word, e.g. *This word begins with 'h', it ends with 'd' and it has 'a' in the middle. What is it?*

If the children find this game easy, vary the order that you give the clues, e.g. *This word has 'a' in the middle, it ends with 'g' and begins with 'b'.*

Assessment (R, AF1) Are the children able to work out the words from the clues you give?

Speaking, listening and drama activities

Objective Retell stories, ordering events using story language (1.2). Listen with sustained concentration (2.1). Ask and answer questions, make relevant contributions, offer suggestions and take turns (3.2).

- Talk about what happened in the story. Ask the children: *What happened at the beginning, in the middle and at the end?*
- Ask the class or group to pretend they haven't heard the story before, then ask a volunteer to tell them the beginning of the story.
- Ask someone else to take over and say what happened next. Then ask a third volunteer to say what happened at the end.
- Praise children for using the past tense and for telling the story in their own words.

Writing activities

Objective Write chronological texts using simple structures (10.1). Compose and write simple sentences independently to communicate meaning (11.1). Write with spaces between words accurately (12.2).

- Ask the children: *Who had new clothes?* Write the names in a line across the board.
- Ask: *What did Biff have?* Draw an arrow from 'Biff' and write 'dress' at the end of the arrow.
- *What happened to the dress?* If necessary, look back at the book to check. Draw an arrow from 'dress' to 'lipstick'.
- Ask the children to draw arrows and say what happened to Chip's shirt and Kipper's top.
- Ask: *What happened after that?* Draw arrows to 'washing machine', then 'lorry'.
- Ask them to write about what happened to one of the children's new clothes, demonstrating how they can use the outline to help them.

Assessment *(W, AF3)* Do the children understand how the outline can help them to sequence the story in the right order? Do they remember to leave spaces between the words?

Look Smart

Tug of War

C = Language comprehension   **R, AF** = QCA reading assessment focus
W = Word recognition   **W, AF** = QCA writing assessment focus

Group or guided reading

Introducing the book

C *(Clarifying)* Read the title and ask the children to tell you what a 'tug of war' is. Ask: *How do you win a tug of war?*

C *(Prediction)* Look at the pictures on pages 14 and 15 to find out who is at each end of the rope. Ask the children to make predictions about what might happen next.

W Read the sentence about the book on the back cover and check that everyone can read the list of high frequency words.

Strategy check

Remind the children to look for clues in the pictures as well as the text.

Independent reading

- Ask the children to read the book on their own from the beginning. Listen to each child in turn. Remind them to use a bookmark or card under the line of text to help them keep their place.

W Encourage the children to sound out new CVC words. Praise them for reading with confidence.

C *(Questioning, Clarifying)* Encourage the children to talk about what is happening in the story.

Assessment Check that the children:
- (R, AF1) recognise names and other high frequency words on sight
- (R, AF3) understand what happened in the story.

Returning to the text

C *(Imagining)* Ask: *Can you think of any other ways that the children might have fooled Mum and Dad into believing they were very strong?*

C *(Clarifying, Imagining)* Ask: *How do you think Mum and Dad feel on page 23?* Ask the children to imagine how they would feel.

C *(Summarising)* Ask the children to retell the story in just two or three sentences.

Group and independent reading activities

Objective Make predictions showing an understanding of ideas, events and characters (7.3).

C *(Questioning, Prediction)* Talk about what happened in the story. Ask:

Why did they decide to skip?

Why do you think they stopped skipping?

Why did Mum and Dad go over the bridge?

Why did all the children let go of the rope, except Kipper?

Why did Mum and Dad fall into the river?

What might Mum and Dad say at the end?

Assessment (R, AF2) Do the children answer the 'why' questions with appropriate reasons?

Objective Apply phonic knowledge and skills as the prime approach to reading and spelling unfamiliar words (5.5).

W **You will need** to cover words that appear in the middle of sentences with reusable stickers, e.g. 'saw' (page 3), 'skip' (page 4), 'began' (page 6), 'too' (page 8), 'over' (page 13).

- Read the story together. When you come to a word that has been covered, ask the children to read past it to the end of the sentence. Think of words that would make sense in the gap.

- Read the sentence again, substituting one of the suggestions for the gap. Ask: *Does it make sense?*
- Peel back the sticker far enough to read the first letter. Ask: *Is that the right letter sound?* Choose a word that makes sense and begins with the correct letter sound. Take away the sticker and read the word.
- Repeat this with each of the missing words.

Assessment (R, AF1) Are they aware if the suggested words make sense or not? Are they able to compare the first letter sounds?

Objective Segment sounds into their constituent phonemes in order to spell them correctly (6.2). Children move from spelling simple CVC words to longer words (6.3).

- **(W)** Make a list of words from the story with initial consonant clusters: 'stream', 'tree', 'skip', 'threw', 'bridge'.
- Choose one of the initial clusters, e.g. 'br'. Ask the children to look through the book to find a word beginning with 'br'. Write it on the board. Ask: *Can you think of any more words that begin with 'br'?*
- Repeat with 'tr', 'sk', 'str' and 'thr'. Find the word in the book each time, then ask the children to think of other examples.

Assessment (R, AF1) Can the children find words that began with each consonant cluster? Can they think of other examples?

Speaking, listening and drama activities

Objective Explore familiar themes and characters through improvisation and role-play (4.1). Act out their own and well-known stories, using voices for characters (4.2).

- Ask the children to act out the tug of war from the time when Wilf's dad throws the rope over the stream, to the end when Mum and Dad fall in.

- Remind the 'Mum' and 'Dad' characters to think about how they would feel if they thought Kipper was stronger than they were.
- Praise children for remembering when it is their turn to say something and for using expression.

Writing activities

Objective Compose and write simple sentences independently to communicate meaning (11.1). Use capital letters and full stops when punctuating simple sentences (11.2). Write most letters, correctly formed and orientated (12.1).

- Ask the children to tell you what happened in this story. Ask: *Whose idea was it to tie the rope to the tractor? Was it a good idea? Who did Wilf have to ask before he tied the rope to the tractor?*
- Ask the children to tell you everything they know about Wilf, e.g. Wilma is his big sister, Chip is his best friend, he has good ideas.
- Ask one of the children to draw Wilf on a large sheet of paper.
- Ask all the children to think of one sentence about Wilf to add to the poster. It can include information that the children have gained from other stories.
- Ask each child to write his/her sentence on the 'What We Know About Wilf' poster.

Assessment *(W, AF3)* Do they use a capital letter to start their sentence and a full stop to end it?

An Important Case

C = Language comprehension   **R, AF** = QCA reading assessment focus
W = Word recognition   **W, AF** = QCA writing assessment focus

Group or guided reading

Introducing the book

W Read the title together. Break down 'important' into phonemes. Ask the children to find shorter words in 'important': *Can you find 'ant'? Can you find 'or' and 'port'?*

- Find the important case in the pictures.
- Read the sentence about the story on the back cover.

C *(Imagining, Prediction)* Ask the children what they think might be in the case. Ask: *What do you think will happen in the story?*

Strategy check

Remind the children to break down longer words to try to make sense of them.

Independent reading

- Ask the children to read the book on their own from the beginning. Listen to each child in turn. Remind them to use a bookmark or card under the line of text to help them keep their place.

W Encourage the children to sound out new CVC words. Prompt as necessary, but give praise for reading with appropriate expression.

W On page 11, praise children for recognising and reading 'important'.

C *(Prediction, Imagining)* Ask: *On page 13, who do you think Dad is calling? What would you do if you found a locked case or bag?*

C *(Summarising)* Ask the children to retell the story in just a few sentences.

Assessment *(R, AF1)* Check that the children can read the list of high frequency words.

Returning to the text

- **(C)** *(Questioning)* Ask the children to describe what is in the thought bubbles and what each child imagines is in the case.
- **(C)** *(Clarifying)* Look at pictures on pages 19–21. Ask: *What clues are there to make Dad think the man is important?* (smart car, chauffeur, bodyguard, the man is wearing a suit, neighbours are looking)

Assessment Check that the children:
- *(R, AF1)* can read high frequency words on sight
- *(R, AF1)* reread sentences if they seem not to make sense.

Group and independent reading activities

Objective Visualise and comment on events, characters and ideas, making imaginative links to their own experiences (8.2).

- **(C)** *(Questioning, Clarifying)* Ask the children to tell you about the important case. Ask: *What did the children think might be inside?*
- Ask: *What was the joke at the end of this story?*
- Remind the children about other books they have read recently, e.g. 'Tug of War'. Ask: *What was the joke at the end of that story?*
- Encourage the children to talk about stories they have enjoyed reading and to say how they ended. Ask: *Did they end with a joke, an 'Oh no!' ending, or a happy ending?*

Assessment *(R, AF3)* Are the children able to talk about other stories and the way they ended?

Objective Use syntax and context when reading for meaning (7.2). Interpret a text by reading aloud with some variety in pace and emphasis (1.3).

- **(C)** *(Clarifying)* Ask the children to find: two full stops on page 1; a comma on page 3; speech marks on page 5; a question mark on page 11.

- Ask a volunteer to read pages 1 and 2. Praise him or her for noticing where sentences end.
- Ask another volunteer to read pages 3–5. Ask them to show that they have noticed where the commas are.
- Encourage other children to read pages 6–9 and 12–15. Ask them to read what people say with expression.
- Ask other children in the group to read the remaining pages. Praise them for using appropriate expression to show full stops, commas, questions and speech.

Assessment *(R, AF3)* Do they use appropriate expression and show an understanding of the context? *(R, AF4)* Are the children aware of punctuation when they read aloud?

Objective Identify the constituent parts of two-syllable and three-syllable words (5.3). Apply phonic knowledge and skills as the prime approach to reading and spelling (5.5). Spell new words using phonics as the prime approach (6.1).

- **(W)** Ask the children to find the longest word in this story ('sandwiches', page 24). Ask: *How did you work out how to read it?* Ask a child to find a shorter word in 'sandwiches'. Break the whole word down into phonemes to read it more easily.
- Ask the children to find words in the story that have more than six letters. Make a list: 'children', 'outside', 'football', 'couldn't', 'important', 'officer'.
- Look at each word in turn. Notice whether there are shorter words inside the longer ones. Write the shorter words beside each longer one, e.g. 'outside': 'out', 'side'.
- Ask for volunteers to try to spell any of the words above. Praise children for having a go at spelling longer words.

Assessment *(R, AF1)* Can the children find shorter words inside longer ones? Do they use this information to spell the longer words?

Speaking, listening and drama activities

Objective Describe incidents from their own experience in an audible voice (1.1). Take turns to speak, listen to others' suggestions and talk about what they are going to do (3.1).

- Ask the children to think of any occasion where they, or someone in their family, found something that wasn't theirs. Ask: *What did you do with it?*
- Describe some situations that might arise, e.g. ask: *If you found a purse on the floor in a supermarket, what would you do with it? If you found a packet of food on a park bench, would you eat it? If you found a glove in the playground at school, what would you do?* Allow time for the children to give their opinions.
- Praise children for listening to each other's ideas, and for not repeating what others have said.

Writing activities

Objective Compose and write simple sentences independently to communicate meaning (11.1). Use capital letters and full stops when punctuating simple sentences (11.2). Write most letters correctly formed and orientated (12.1).

- Talk about what happened in this story. Ask: *How did it begin? Who found the case? What did Dad do? Who came to collect it? What was in the case?*
- Ask the children to write four or five sentences about the story.
- Remind the children that every sentence needs to begin with a capital letter and end with a full stop.
- Ask the children to read their sentences to the class or group. Ask: *Does each sentence make sense? Does each sentence end with a full stop?*

Assessment (W, AF2) Do the children write legibly and with the correct pencil hold?
(W, AF3) Do their sentences follow the sequence of the story?

INSPIRATIONAL SUPPORT FOR TEACHERS
For free professional development videos from leading experts, plus other resources and free eBooks, please go to
www.oxfordprimary.co.uk

HELPING YOU ENGAGE PARENTS
We have researched the most common concerns and worries parents have about their children's literacy and provide answers and support in
www.oxfordowl.co.uk
This site contains advice on how to share a book, how to pronounce pure sounds, how to encourage boys' reading, and much more. We hope you will find the site useful and recommend it to your parents.

OXFORD
UNIVERSITY PRESS

Great Clarendon Street, Oxford OX2 6DP

Oxford University Press is a department of the University of Oxford. It furthers the University's objective of excellence in research, scholarship, and education by publishing worldwide in

Oxford   New York
Auckland   Cape Town   Dar es Salaam   Hong Kong   Karachi
Kuala Lumpur   Madrid   Melbourne   Mexico City   Nairobi
New Delhi   Shanghai   Taipei   Toronto

With offices in

Argentina   Austria   Brazil   Chile   Czech Republic   France
Greece   Guatemala   Hungary   Italy   Japan   Poland
Portugal   Singapore   South Korea   Switzerland
Thailand   Turkey   Ukraine   Vietnam

Oxford is a registered trade mark of Oxford University Press in the UK and in certain other countries

Text © Oxford University Press 2008

Written by Pam Mayo, based on the orginal characters created by Roderick Hunt and Alex Brychta.

The moral rights of the author have been asserted

Database right Oxford University Press (maker)

First published 2008
This edition published 2011

All rights reserved. No part of this publication may be reproduced, stored in a retrieval system, or transmitted, in any form or by any means, without the prior permission in writing of Oxford University Press, or as expressly permitted by law, or under terms agreed with the appropriate reprographics rights organization. Enquiries concerning reproduction outside the scope of the above should be sent to the Rights Department, Oxford University Press, at the address above

You must not circulate this book in any other binding or cover and you must impose this same condition on any acquirer

British Library Cataloguing in Publication Data

Data available

Cover illustrations Alex Brychta

ISBN: 978-0-19-848240-6

10 9 8 7 6 5 4 3

Page make-up by Thomson Digital

Printed in China by Imago

Paper used in the production of this book is a natural, recyclable product made from wood grown in sustainable forests. The manufacturing process conforms to the environmental regulations of the country of origin.